My Book of ABC

Picture book

INTRODUCE THE ALPHABET TO TODDLERS

From A to Z, each page introduces the next letter sound with familiar objects that will engage your toddler and make early learning simple and fun!

A a
apple

B b

bear

cat

Dd

duck

E e

elephant

F f

frog

G g

goat

H h

hedgehog

igloo

J j

jam

K k

kangaroo

L l

lion

monkey

N n

nest

orange

pig

Q q

queen

R r

racoon

S s

sheep

T t

turtle

umbrella

V v

violin

W w

watermelon

X x

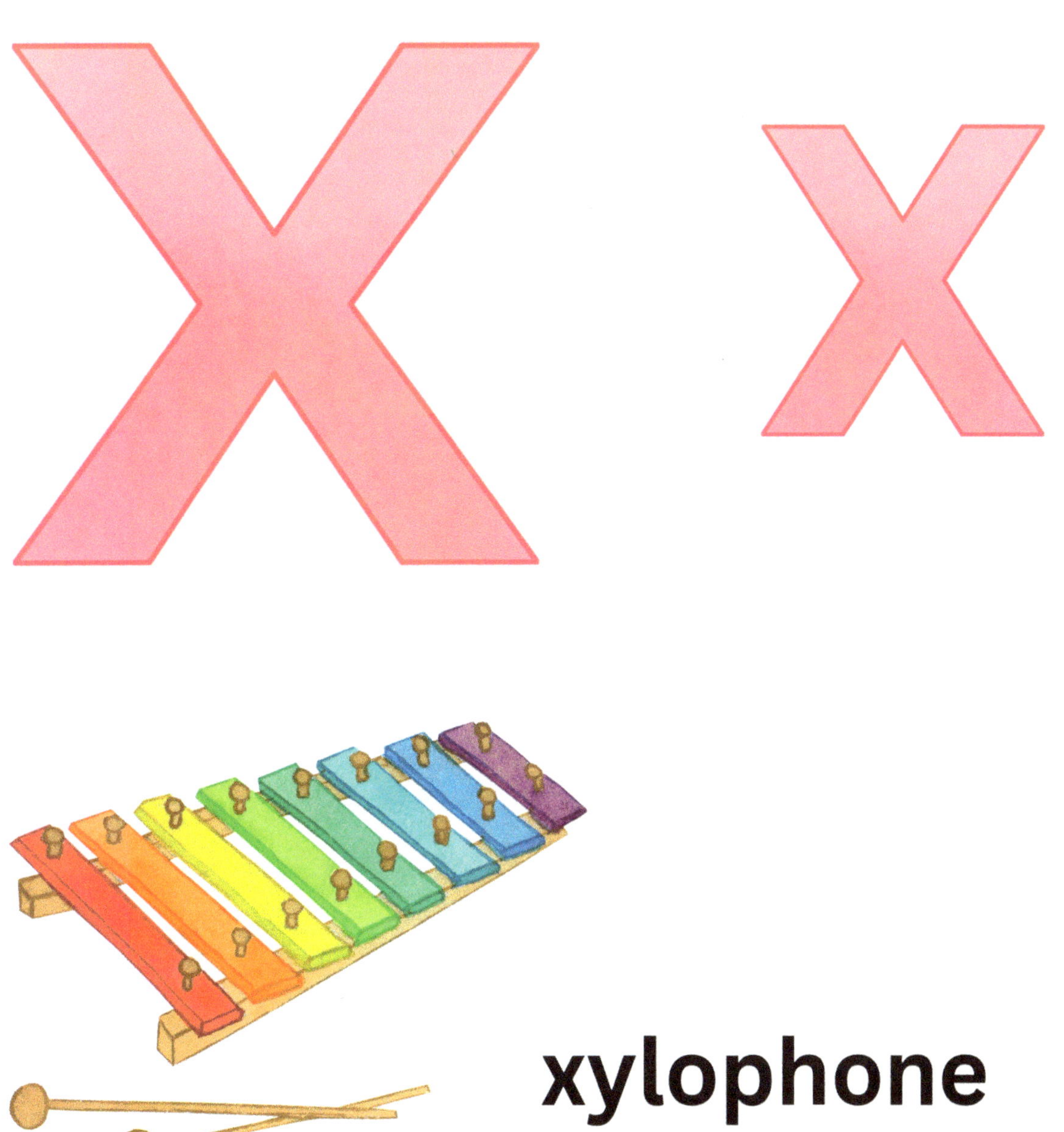

xylophone

yoyo

Z z

zebra